HER PSALMS

HER PSALMS

A Song of Triumph

KASHIYA LESTER

Kashiyavici

GOD,

GRANT ME THE WORDS.

This Moon Baby,
He made me crave his cheeks.

Son, You are the greatest star it has been my pleasure to birth. I only know God because of You. I am a god because of You. It has been the honor of a lifetime to witness You, a god, evolve.

Mommy

I was crucified for being a star;
A nature I never asked for.
Only to ascend; my home, afar.
To Celestials awakening my form.

Ousted into the shadows,
For my good, only God knows.
I educated myself amongst the fellows,
Only to learn I was meant to let go.

For I would never become a star
In those shadows. Light was exposed through my
scars.
And I broke free— after oh so many wars,
I found my home... Amongst my fellows...
Amongst the stars.

Tell them the gods and goddesses they warned You about are here.

For the better part of our lives, many of us knew The Bible to be a book of law. If there ever needed to be a final say in the rules of life, we knew where the answer could be found. We, also, knew that the law would come from the mouths of men. The consideration of women would only come after the man was heard. It, still, amazes Me that millions of people never questioned the belief that Woman came from a man's rib, then women took the reins from there.

This book is not to debate beliefs. This book is not meant to address any religion, nor way or life. But a book of journeys is valid from any source. A book infused with wisdom, art, love, and empowerment, can be just as influential and transformative as Corinthians, Proverbs, or Revelations.

For are we not descendants of God? Have we not endured adventures and situations that have made us better? Do we not tap into our intuition, and reside in different dimensions, as we figure out this thing called life?

The greatest storms are named after women. The greatest sources embody the feminine spirit: Mother Earth, Mother nature... Mother Africa. How have we allowed the narrative of life to be stolen from us, when we are the epitome of Life?

'Her Psalms' is our tale. It is the song cry of an ascended daughter. Our life literature is our scripture, and it is just as significant as those of men. As far as I'm concerned, the voice of a woman is most valid-- especially when blessings flow from our truth alone. Are we not the ones to carry the load? Do we not bear, and birth, the pain of the world? When we are there for everyone, and no one is there for us, yet we still make a way, is that not the very makings of a heroine? Is it not our fault, and our fight, all at the same time?

Had we been given the podium from the beginning, society may not be so imbalanced. If we were encouraged to share our scars, as well as our remedies, we could have saved so many from emergency rooms.

"I need my sister's song as much as I need mine. This is her story. This is her Psalms."

Je Ne Regrette Rein
I Regret Nothing.

HER PSALMS

"This is her story. This is her psalms."

Black Girl,

Please, secure your own mask before attempting
to help your neighbor.

The fog is temporary
At least I'm in motion
The view is murky
At least I am floating

Foolish of Me to expect a guideline
To the life that I dreamed, on a path that is only mine

I apologize to Self for inflicting guilt wounds
By following the steps of those who gave up too soon
For what do they know about success when all they
discuss and manifest is doom?

I check myself before wreckage
I expose my pain and free myself from blockage

Though up and down, uncomfortable, and maddening
Not a force in Hell can stop my growth from
happening

If everything was easy and clear; black and white
I wouldn't have much of a story for this mission

I shall have my blue skies, all in due time
Until then, witness my honorable, cloudy transition

Matriculation

Remember walking into class and being hit with a
pop quiz that You, totally, weren't expecting? That is
what those tough lessons are. Just think of yourself in
a season of classes when those moments arrive.
Sometimes, You're due for a quiz: You're being
challenged on what You know, while, simultaneously,
being put in a situation to use what You know,
therefore, actually implementing the lesson in Life.

"So You raised the bar, huh? You're on a new level?
You said You've raised your standards...
You said You won't stand for this and that anymore.
Well... Let's See!"

Lay the boulder of Ego waste side.
The grounding of Wisdom is much more divine.
And as You sacrifice, in the face of Obedience,
Reside in Peace... What is yours is mine.
Asé.

Her Psalms | 001

Higher Grounding

I realized the ego residing within my spirituality:
For a while, I was reluctant to take on more spiritual
meditative practices. Not, necessarily, defiant, but,
steadily, doing what suited Me. I was comfortable, yes,
but I wasn't growing. That, alone, is blocking Blessings.
It is, still, resistance, no matter the form.

There's no way that I could ever receive more without
honoring God more. The energy exchange is ever-
fueling one another. The effort must be reciprocal...
How could I forget this? The nerve! I was quite serious
when I said that I was ready to face anything in my
way. This includes kicking myself in the ass if need be.

The chin-check was necessary: If You're not going to
be accountable to Yourself, You sure aren't going to be
responsible for Yourself, in front of anyone else.

I agree to increase my praise,
My grounding, my discipline,
In alignment with increase of
My blessings, my recognitions,
My rewards, and Abundance.
All will flow with Ascension.
Asé.

Her Psalms | 002

Decisions

It's my decision. To which shall I bind?
What will I bring to the forefront of my mind?
What will I let lead? What will be My Truth:
"Can I do this? It's all too much. I'm passed my youth..."
Or
"I've got this. However I do it, that's how it should be done.
I'm handling this— and very well, I might add. I've already
won.
I am right on time. Everything is more than fine.
Nothing that is for Me will pass Me. I am aligned."

Which Truth will be mine?
In which Truth will I reside?

Who has the power?
Where is the power?
Why isn't Power in Me, right now, in this hour?
If I breathe it in, do I feel more at peace?
If Peace is here, why should it cease?
... What else is there to go back and forth about?
It isn't Me vs. Me, but Me vs. Doubt.

Even if Doubt doth creep, I'll let this process be my Peace;
I shall breathe in the power of my own decree.
Remember the scoreboard. This isn't a bet.
The Promise hasn't failed Me yet.

And it never will.

Hell all around Me.
I am calm.
Living in the Now is my balm.

I am not Anxiety.
I know the future.
To control, I stopped trying.
The Now is my suture.

I am not Depression.
I can't fix the past.
I stopped the obsession.
It sure as shit didn't last.

Still, Hell all around Me.
Demons that just won't get gone.
But for now, I'll keep my peace.
Hell can wait until dawn.

Her Psalms | 003

I rebuke the spirit of feeling unworthy,
guilty, ashamed, and incapable of love,
all because of
Gaslighting by a weak individual.
Yes, it hurt. Yes, I have to process it.
Yes, I am healing, but I'm still handling it.
Because I am worthy.

Her Psalms | 004

If I cut my skin
And exposed all that is within
I would be forced to reveal my greatest, deepest sin

Here I lie: a liar
Stuck by no one else than who I was prior

In my head, dying over and over again
From the Me of before, and all of her pain

And that bleeding bitch chants "I can't... I just can't."
And I believe her; mourning aggressively, with the
nerve to rant

All I have to do is change
I already know I cannot stay the same

But my laziness from crippling fear
Wins the award for best supporting actor of the year

I cannot die before I wake
I need a god to help me shake
I need a magic beyond my control
To overpower my crippled soul

My gifted spirit, a bloody hostage
As I excuse this suicide of self-sabotage

Healing the mess within You makes room for all of You: all that which is in agreement with your best interest; your best self. Being full of You strengthens your spirit of discernment. Having a solid, stable, grounded spirit of discernment means that no one can shake your security. When no one can shake your security, You do not second guess the respect You deserve. When the proposition of less is extended, You will not hesitate to refuse it. You will be certain of what You deserve, and certain when You are not getting it. You can cut things right there.

Sure, You will be called everything but Queen, even while You stand up for yourself, but at least the standard has been set. Anyone who takes offense to the fact that You refuse to be offended is a disrespectful individual who only benefitted off of offending You. Their season is over.

At the end of the day, You did not compromise yourself just to appease someone who never planned on honoring You— because You shouldn't have had to compromise in the first place. You might feel some type of way because that person won't be happy, but You honored yourself! After a while, You won't hesitate at all... You won't feel bad for addressing someone who made it clear that they sought to belittle You. Once it is clear that they fully understand You, but choose to diminish what You said in order to focus on their own desires, You owe them nothing more

Some say that it is up to women to change the way that the world treats us... Those same people will turn around and tell us we're everything but queens for actually taking matters into our own hands, and demanding better treatment. They don't care. They just want us to hush.

But how much has it benefited You to bite your tongue for "the greater good"? How long have You allowed things to eat You alive, all alone, internally, because You thought about the other person's feelings, even after they, clearly, didn't think about yours? Was it, really, all good?

The disrespect is done.
The belittling is done.
The manipulation is done.
The placating and gaslighting is done.
The disregard that we live and breathe and feel too— is done.
The expectation that You will sacrifice yourself
for everyone else is done.
Done, done, and done.
Asé.

Her Psalms | 005

Somewhere down the line,
I dropped my self worth to love You.
Then, when I picked it up,
You punished Me for it.

I HAVE PEACE DURING THE BATTLE
BECAUSE I HAVE ALREADY WON THE WAR.

Word War I

I'll take my frustrations out with these words,
Beat the fuck out of this defeatist energy with my
verbs,
Kick the teeth in, with my spelling, of those who try
to curse,
Recall and call in Blessings that contradict the worst.

I'll slap the shit out the these spiritual attacks with
my syntax,
Strangle the spirit of the damned before my bless'ed
downpour comes in next,
Throw a brick at the windows closed to Me with my
dialect,
And dowse the place with my gasoline text
Before I light this bitch on fire with my intellect.

I'll stop your conjuring with my own sentence summoning,
Send my Ancestors to completely sink You with the stories I have coming,
Reverse your very work with my wordage— because, clearly, You're dumb-and
Trying Me? Sweetheart, start running.

I'll no longer be the savage that came with so much baggage.
Goddess level-living means I'm an alchemist just by offering an adage.
My divine dialogue delivers deadly damage.
So effective, nothing You try will ever be able to manage.

My terms alone could bless your bones.
Instead, You wanted to bitch and moan.
So the leniency I lent will leave You alone.
Let my English usher You into your new doomed home.

I call in the spirits of Happiness and Prosperity.
I rebuke imposter syndrome.
I call out the heaviness and burden, unjustly, put on Me
which led Me to not even consider all that I deserve.
I am Luxuriance.
I summon Affluence...
Now.
I conjure Wealth. I am allowed to be lavished.
Asé.

 Her Psalms | 006

What the World Needs Now

There's so much Love and Respect missing from the world:

No space for human error,
No accountability for human terror,
No consideration for human evolution,
No responsibility in relationships, therefore, no solutions,
Too much unaddressed drama,
Refusal to resolve childhood trauma,
Disrespectfully dumping problems on "loved ones",
Then blaming them for their attempt to rid their selves of the energy when people are done,
No one able to converse, even with articulation,
So much Love lost from lack of communication,
So much wisdom lost from the lack of connection,
So much hurt and painful energy manifested because no one can transmutate,

Honest communication replaced by
people trying to project, gaslight, and manipulate,
So many fleeting distractions,
Survival competitions, fashion labels, and lies
to compensate for the lack of action,
High extremes of insecurity from the lack of "wins",
High debts in society because of material things,
All the loss that has replaced Love and Respect
Fallacies,
Fears,
Fronting,
Fakes...

All of it we will, certainly, regret.

If I am to be misunderstood,
then I shall be so only amongst the wrong crowds.
If I am to be defensive,
then I will be so only in the wrong locations.
If I am to be restricted,
then I shall be so only within the wrong establishments.

I only know discomfort by recognizing comfort.

I gained Understanding amongst the right crowds.
I felt Acceptance in the right places.
I am Free as I Expand and Ascend.
The discomfort led Me to the Level meant for Me.

Her Psalms | 007

Your Spirit of Discernment is more important than You realize.
That little voice in your head could be anything in disguise:
Could be Ego.
Could be Pride.
Could be Depression.
Could be right.
But your Spirit of Discernment will always let You know.
When You need to know the truth, it will, surely tell You so.
It is your protector. Your compass.
Your healing. Your success.

Strengthen your Spirit of Discernment.
... God will do the rest.

It will take every triggered nerve,
every tremble in your voice,
every butterfly in your belly,
and every rejoicing ancestor, for you to say
"No, I'm not doing this anymore."

Speak Over Yourself

I am NOT the narcissist just because a narcissist
projected onto Me.
I do not move in ill intent.
I do not manipulate.
I do not usher in confusion, conflict, nor chaos.
I am not an energy vampire.
My Love is pure.
My intentions are sincere.
My psyche will not succumb to their attack.
My reaction was not the cause. It was the effect.
I will not be the scapegoat for someone else's
problems.
I do not resonate with the hatred spoken on Me.
I return the lies to its sender. I return the guilt to its
sender.
I will not deconstruct myself because that person
refuses to heal and rebuild.
The way I defend myself, after being attacked,
is my accountability to accept.
I will not embody their karma.
I release unwarranted guilt.
I release unwarranted guilt.
I release unwarranted guilt.
I am not their lies. I am my truth.
I don't need to be absolved of their lies,
in order to feel acceptable.

Speak Over Yourself

I don't need acceptance from someone that chose
not to do right by Me again & again.
I am not looking to be forgiven by someone
who should beg for my forgiveness.
I am not responsible for their hell.
I am open to Love, even when I don't feel lovable.
I know that putting up walls not only keep Love out,
but they keep Abundance from flowing in.
Love is Abundance.
I am committed to Betterment.
When every atom in my body wants to shut down
and accept all the frustration and pain as my identifier,
I promise to speak Love into myself.
I will not be the very saboteur of my Blessings.
The Universe will not hear my pain as my prayers.
My promise is more lucrative than that.
When compared to my goals, my complaints are
meaningless.
I am not a complainer. I am not the victim.
My Appreciation is my Manifestation.
There is always something to be thankful for.
There is always a silver lining.
Even when I can't see it, I'm already good.
I reside in positive, affirming energy, knowing that I already
win.

Asé.

Does It?

Doesn't it hurt You to stay in small places?
Does your body not ache from being so restricted?
Do You not fill with rage from a cage far too small?
Does the frustration from needing Freedom not get to
You?

Does it?

Her ego shames her heart for its sentiment:
 "How did We forget ourself— for simple men?
We've seen Queens precede us and plea:
Sacrifice romance. Save your sanity.
And You cracked my crown for a clown?
Sis... You've let us down."

I thought I wanted a lover, but my spirit wasn't
settled.
It wasn't a person, but it was something.
After some extended time alone, and intentional,
tender digging,
I realized that it was a passion for Life I was
missing...
I crave a jolt to my system,
just confused which spot needed caressing.
The fulfillment isn't as simple as a body.
Not as rudimentary as mutual undressing.

I have a calling all on my own.
Man came from my womb. I am not made from his
rib bone.
My own calling needs Me to answer the phone.
My own spirit needs Me to be its home.

I don't want a break.
I don't need a break.
I do not wish to be broken.
I want Rest. I desire Peace.
I command relaxation and replenishment.
I call in positive, beneficial forces that make
my very active, very healthy and capable life
easier.
I welcome the resources to ease my stress and
workload.
I manifest large sums of money
from multiple sources of income
to flow easily into my life.
I am ready for lavish gifts and vacations.
I accept, and flow with ascension, to my
season of acknowledgment and reward.
And so it is.

Her Psalms | 008

Hiding Hell

At this point of my journey,
I can feel my ego being an entity outside of myself,
literally.
I know when this bitch is ready to take the stage.
I know the icky feeling when She wants to
misbehave.
I even recognize the heaviness when She has the
reins.
I recognize myself away from Detriment.
A gracious graduation... A successful new age.

We can sense the ego shift in others as well.
It's very obvious who takes the wheel of their Hell,
In a physical human vehicle,
At any given moment, time will tell:
Their voice changes,
Their offered comprehension changes—
Even their eyes change... It's sadly strange.

No one thinks they show their Hell.
Everyone believes they're hiding their Hell so well
(I know I like to believe so, but it's only Ego's veil)...
Meanwhile, we're a whole mess, inside and out,
And it's extremely obvious
to those who aren't impressed by clout.
If I could scream... If I could shout,
From Me to Me, I'd say so loud:
"You're not okay! Please, stop being so proud!
Drop the facade
before it eats Us Alive!"

I WILL, GLADLY, LET GO OF YOU,
JUST TO STEP INTO THE GREATNESS
FOR WHICH I AM MEANT.

God Said: " You won't get it until You get it for yourself.
I made You 'It'... Not anyone else.
No one else will lead,
intercede,
nor help You with your chores.
I made It all for You, so no man can claim what is yours.
Everything waits on You.
Everyone else comes after You...

Let Me make it easier for You:
Your name is now 'Gift'.
Walk as such."

Okay, God... I hear You.

I LOVE YOU, BUT I WILL LET YOU
LEAVE.
I CANNOT COME DOWN. I AM DOING A
GREAT WORK.

My spirit cannot be seduced into going backwards.
My flesh needed coercion in the past,
But it is not navigating this ship anymore.
Beckon Me, summon Me,
Pray for Me, call my name...
Do what You want.
I hear it all— behind Me.

And I'm not going that way.

This journey led Me to an understanding, and commitment, to Myself. As I healed, I understood that it was not only necessary to remember the good words, but it was imperative to be disciplined with them.

Implementation, which is Manifestation itself, is the only true way to honor yourself.

"If I am to be a Goddess, let Me walk as such."

Her Psalms | 009

Hey, solo butterfly
Your box is so wide
Ample space to be wild in,
with no one else inside

Hey solo butterfly
Setting the stage on fire
Governing over the fields You gallop in,
Hiding in public, from their eye

Don't You know the world will wait as long as You
will hide?
.... When will You come out from the inside?

Lol...
It does look crazy:
Me, fighting battles, while I'm cradled in God's arms.

Many times,
Standing up for yourself means standing alone,
by yourself.
Don't worry, these are the best conditions to fly in.

It's been hard to express,
And flex,
The best of my best,
Because of an invalid shame that I've placed on
myself.

I felt bad for being great.
Even though it's my natural state.
I felt misplaced in a state which put Me in a place that
disgraced my grace when I tried to take the stage.
I suffocated in locations
With people happy to take and take.
'Long as there weren't any tables I tried to shake.

When the world lost its saturation,
I brought in coloration.
And was told my representation was too much for
any adequate collaboration.
... I grew gray and called it Maturation.

After all the gaslighting and careful conditioning.
I was left wishing
That I could shine— nay, glisten:
Glisten and galvanize like the goddesses that didn't
listen.
What did they possess that I could've been missing?

When I heard the words I blurted, it was like I hit a curb.
My vehicle needed maintenance just to implement a verb:

"They didn't listen."
That was the mission.
That was the key I needed in my ignition.

They lied when they said I had to do it for man.
Lied again when they said I couldn't do it, when I can.
Took my essence and sold it back to Me in a sketchy van.
I should've known that this was not divine femininity's plan.

I checked the manual to the goddess I am learning to be.
This one section read: "Repeat after Me:
If it feels real to Me, it is right for Me.
If I unlearn and tap in, I'll be the best of Me.
Remove toxicity.
Fill up with divinity.
Divest from this wicked world: ... Garden thee."

I thought to myself and myself spoke:
"You are a voice that is meant to provoke.
You are detached yet emotional,
Ambitious yet inflexible,
A tower, yet vulnerable.
In the past, these traits got You in a lot of trouble,
Now evolved, they are pivotal.
You were meant to change the world.
You are no ordinary girl.
Take what You've learned,
Do not shun what You've earned.
Be the trouble that they need.
We need You to succeed.

Don't fear the critiques
Your wrongs are right... Beloved, be free."

Her Psalms | 009

Settle for the pain of being right.
Let your faith be your Power.
Let your own validation be your Might.

God,

Set my success up next.
No more sacrificing myself.
Time to hang up happy memories;
Put past possibilities on a shelf.

Help Me call back in my Power.
Surely, it is passed pity hour.
If I can produce this dopamine
from a pipe dream
then the product isn't in the piping.

I offer my romantic reverie
In exchange for obtainable fantasies.
... Surely my imagination is of better use
than what it, currently, seems.

Help me rebuild. This time, not in vain.
... Love is a losing game.
Should us two meet again,
Let that moment be divine; in your name.
Asé.

Her Psalms | 010

Loving myself means
being committed to the betterment of myself at all times.
I am active in Life. I am mindful every minute.
Even though there are times to welcome the emotions,
and feel them in order to release,
I still made a promise to myself to do the work. 25/8
As I loved myself, I found it best practice
to commit to always creating positivity.
That means shutting down thoughts
that can manifest those things I crave no more.
I AM MY DUTY.
I will, always, remember the honor that I am;
— that I deserve,
and bring nothing but Honor to myself.
No more will I relish in the valleys.
I do not pity myself; digging myself deeper
into everything I complain about.
Power is in my tongue. It's in my thoughts.
It's in my mindset. It's what I allow.
MY POWER IS WHAT I ALLOW.
And I no longer allow myself Hell on Earth.

My eye-line adjusted, redirected to the hills
My crown profoundly revealed.
I feel chills, remembering the deal
I take these affirmations like pills
I heal
I remember who I am and I chill
I create what is real.

And so it is.

Her Psalms | 011

I kept going.
Today, I wanted to die.
Instead, I kept going.

Look at that: I kept going.

Just as sure as I am of my next breath,
I am certain that the universe will provide the rest.
... I am not a mess.
In fact, I'm quite blessed.

I am fortunate,
Favored,
Lucky,
unwavered.

I have peace.
I have power.
In magic, I shower.

I have grace.
I am regal.
Flexing this well should be illegal.

I have confidence
I defeat fear.
And I conquered the hell out of this last year,

I am an alchemist.
I change states.
Look how I went from bad, to better, to great.

Nothing I accept can have Power
over Me until I allow it to.
Nothing foreign to my truth
can affect Me and my progress.
There is no delay, only advancement.
Asé.

This will end like I want it to. I win.
The enemy will have to lose again.
See, I'm a different fighter now.
And I have God to thank.
'Cause God's joy is my strength.

Crown of Glory

"I knew I was over the real heavy healing when I no
longer wanted to cut and color my hair."

Even little girls grab a pair of scissors to gain control.
Isn't it deep? Even in adolescence, a girl's queendom
screams to her within: "I am not to be controlled. I can
be taught. I can be guided. I can even be raised. But
don't You dare try to control Me."
When we're bored, when it's over, when the seasons
change— but life hasn't in a while, we seek makeovers.
Not just makeovers; mental-altering, drastic measures.
We must regain some of the control we've seemed to
have lost somewhere along the way: "When did life
become so dull?" "Why am I not seeing results yet?"
... "Where did it all go wrong?"

Whatever leads us towards the bleach and the scissors,
It is proof of Transition. We are seeking to make our
outsides match our inside:
Be it chaotic, escaping a cocoon, or a successful
leveling up.

In the attempt to keep my crown balanced, I got creative.
It got a bit destructive,
But even that was progressive.
When they came for my crown, I caught their call,
And took back control.

Color Me Mine.

Her Psalm | 012

Mirror Magic

You have been special
and favored
your entire life;
feeling like You were one of a kind,

but had no true confirmation
until You met another one
of your kind.

Meet Yourself

She sighed.
... Happily, she cried.
See, the tears were justified this time,
Because, this time, they were divine.

She moaned.
Filled in the moment— all alone.
All alone, Transcendence was hers to own.
Scorned and torn, but whole and grown.
She was proud of the scars she adorned.

She has always been the epitome of Her.
Everything that she is, she is all of it.
You will do yourself a great disservice
by trying to fit her into one category.
Don't define her.
She is just Her...
And, boy, does she execute Her so perfectly.

Her Psalms | 013

I, free spirit
Turned off by control. Acceptance unrequited
Desiring nothing but happy elevation
Needing separation to achieve reparation
Only peace can serve Me
Purpose over popularity
Alas, I am privileged
Victorious even without a village
It has made me a black hippie
I am, finally, Peace

Her Psalms | 014

Say my name.
Say it with every muscle.
Say it with intent, not a lazy struggle.
Honor the gift God gave You and enunciate.
It'll bless your taste buds if You dedicate:
Christen the "Kuh", get carried away...
Let my "SHY" send shivers down your spine.
Exalt the "Yuh" like You call in Yahweh.
Call Me with Love... My title is so divine.

It's not Tchaikovsky
Or even Oppenheimer.
It is simple yet sovereign, like an exquisite flower.
It is vibrant and unique,
Quite powerful with technique.
Say it proudly and say it well,
Or I'll constantly critique.
Whether it's Sarah or Suzanne,
I deserve the respect.
Say my name like I know you can.
I expect nothing less.

I Am

I am great.
I am doing my best.
I am not behind... I am passing my tests.

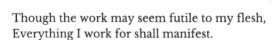

I am better than what I see:
Succeeding, even when I can't see
The forest for the trees.

Though the work may seem futile to my flesh,
Everything I work for shall manifest.

I am the bomb.
..... add the ".com"

I am all that and a bag of chips.
The luxurious life is begging me to take a dip.

Miracular flows through my blood.
I am divinely gifted from above.
I see abundance making its way to me
and I already know it fits me like a glove.

I am appreciative of what I have now.
I could have less but I have more than enough somehow.

Hey Goddess,
I see You in class,
Unlearning everything and flourishing fast.
Embodying excellence, watering your grass.
Doing everything You can to make sure You pass.

Hey Queen,
I've noticed.
You're doing your thing:
Grabbing mental clarity, your power— everything.
I hear the confidence that has entered your speaking.
I can tell that healing has changed your thinking.

Sis,
You beautiful, blessed gift.
I want You to act like You are the shit.
There's a sovereignty You wear that no one else can fit.
Let them try, let them squeeze— it won't matter one bit.
Beloved, this is for You. Listen to these last lines:

Nothing that is for You is lost in this lifetime
Even if You can't tell, everything is already fine.
You are learning to align.
And, damn it, that is so divine.

If my words be magic, then, in them, I will be glad.
Let my mouth speak miracles in myriad.
My dictation delivers downpours of dowries.
Overflows of fortune... Precipitation of pleasantries.
If I am to birth a blessed breath, then let beauty bestow Me.
Bind Me to delight. Pair Me with Peace.
My language is luck. I flourish in favor.
I spoke an existence that was something to savor.

Her Psalms | 015

There are plenty of people who came just to get something from Me, without offering anything, or even less: Penis.
I release all of those users.

There are people who find Me so intriguing and want to be close to Me just to say they got the chance to play in my head.

I detach from those vampires. There are people, right now, who are formulating ways to get in my energy, my presence, my mind, my money, and my blessings. They don't want to bless Me. They want to take and ruin. I stop their formulation and send their intents, curses, and hexes back to them tenfold.

I manifest honest people. I manifest pure people. I manifest people who fully understand that they're extraordinary, know that they're destined for greatness, and are not afraid of it. I call in people who are ready to be extraordinary with Me. I call in successful people, authentic people, divine people.

I welcome sincere people,
people who genuinely see Me,
people who fuel Me, people who replenish Me,
people who cherish Me, people who are considerate of Me, people who are eager to bless Me, people who understand Love, people who want to give, just as much as I want to give. People who are for Me.

Asé.

Spiritually,
She surpassed him twice over.
She faced her Hell... Her most painful seasons
behind her.
Wise as she was, she saw his Hell on the way.
Loving as she was, she thought she could save
him from that day.
Love— she was... She wanted to stop his fall.
She'd protect everyone if she could...
She'd absolutely give her all.
If only they'd let her.
If only he'd let her.
But Hell is personal:
A terrible rite of passage... Cruel, yet essential.
So she resides in her Heaven, alone but aware:
He will get through his Hell.
God won't give him more than he can bear.

International Women's Day

"Why,
I think this world could use a little more
of women being selfish.
And why not?
So far,
Taking care of everyone else
has not bore much fruit for ourselves.

What if, darling— what if we washed our hands—
And did what we wanted to first?

Why,
The world would crumble before we even got a turn."

They've been telling women like Me to calm down
since the beginning of time:
Don't be so confident. Don't take up space.
Don't consider yourself. Don't be fearless.
Don't be vocal. Don't be too intelligent.
Don't acknowledge your power.
Don't demand respect. Don't know your worth.

They've been telling women like Me to calm down
since the beginning of time:
Slow down. Be quiet. Relax
Be seen, not heard. Be coiffed.
Compete with her.
Stand behind him.
Be Second. Expect less.
You're too much.
Beauty OR brains... Not both.

They've been telling women like Me to calm down
since the beginning of time:
That's why You know about Adam and Eve,
and not Adam and Lilith.
That's why Medusa got a bad rep.
That's why Black Women are vilified first, and validated
last.
That's why we're called "Crazy" before we're called
"Queen".
That's why God is, also, called "He".

They've been telling women like Me to calm down
since the beginning of time:
And ain't nothing changed.
No matter how many times we heal You,
Birth You, Help You, Rebuild You, Bankroll You,
Influence You, Support You,
Ghostwrite You, Love You, or save You.

They've been telling women like Me to calm down
since the beginning of time:
But if we listened,
They would surely die.

You can call Me:
Goddess
Conqueror
Gorgeous
Blessed

Madam
Grace
Your Highness
Empress

Rebel
Teach'
Phoenix
Rich Ass Bitch

Heiress
Ascended
Prosperous
Mended

They lied, Sis...
They've been lying for years.

Being extraordinary comes natural to You,
and since You were born,
there were programs performed.
There's been agents around,
Trying to get You to "settle down".

They've applied pressure, Sis.
They haven't let up a bit.

They've muted your individuality
to create an assembly
that told You not to believe in your being:
"... We'll do the heavy lifting".

That's why it's so hard to believe in You:
It was done on purpose, Boo.

"Give Me your Power, for Acceptance for an hour.
I'll remind You that You're, kind of, good,
long as You don't wake up to it too.
I've been working on You for years:
when I noticed that You could do
what I can't do"

What was it they saw?
Why do they envy your grass?
Girl, your ass can sway and shift the masses.
You influence rooms without anyone having to ask.
BEAUTIFUL! The way You bask in your light should be a class.

Divinity rolls off your tongue.
Power flows through your lungs.
And what they can't get over is—
You never asked for these gifts...
... Not even one.
... And they were too lazy to find out what they can get done
so they diminished your ISness:
"Keep quiet, stay barefoot and have my Son."

See, You can't manifest
if You think You can't pass the tests.
You'll never be abundant
If You're constantly running from judgement.
You'll never feel like You're "enough"
If they're feeding You lies in order to buy their
stuff.

Your power was snatched.
This is Chess: game, set, match.

I promise there's magic in between your hips.
Swing, switch... Let them beg for a sip.
I swear You have power right on your lips
Speak. Summon... Your words are honey: let 'em
drip.

I am certain that You birth bounty.
You blessed Muse, they long for your anointing.

Call your essence back to its residence.
It's never too misplaced for You to embrace.

Lies bear no weight
on a woman that is great.

And even if it takes some time
to see how You have always been divine,
That is just fine.

... The world is in trouble once You finally align.

Why should I aspire to YOUR standards of
excellence?
You are known for making mediocrity and calling
it a present.
You already are the weaker people as history will
tell it.
And, instead of raising the bar, You shame and
discredit.

So why would ANYTHING that You do—
Be something that I should aspire to?
I lap You in majesty. You're still in pursuit.
I am superior and I am sacred. I could teach You a
thing or two.

I am so proud of myself.
I didn't put myself on the shelf.
It's been hard as hell and I still didn't ask for help.

It's hard to believe: I finally did it.
Despite it all, I didn't quit.
And even when I lost it all, failure just didn't fit.

Look at Me, I made it through.
I actually won. I didn't lose.
So this isn't for Me as much as it is for You:

If I did it, You can too.

Life Ledger

Buy a journal with a cover You admire.
Buy a pen that keeps You inspired.
Carry them wherever You go.
Wherever your passion is, I, God, will follow.

Write.
Write anything.
Let your pen sing.
Write beautiful and beastly things.
Write words of Love that come to mind
whenever You think of Me.
They shall be seeds. Pen Our Legacy.

Find some sage'and—
Seal it between the pages.
Let your words free You from your mental cages.

Take photos.
Candid, soul-defining photos.
Combine it all into a literature show.
Marvel at the riddles You have scribbled alive.
This baby You've delivered means You'll always
survive.

And when You're ready.
When You're ready to switch.
Your Love and the journal,
For Me and forever,
Come to Me,
And We,
Finally, shall be.

I'm thankful You're still here.
Especially after this year.
I'm thankful there's still another day, even if it
starts with fear.

I'm thankful the world hasn't conquered You yet.
God knows we didn't deserve any of the turmoil
we met.
There are forces out there that You, still, don't
know of yet.
And You're still equipped to face them— still able
to find rest.

I appreciate the way You try— every single day.
I'm so glad that, through everything, You always
find a way.

I'm happy that the darkness didn't overshadow
your sun.
Even if there's overcast; it's another day begun.

And even when the news got worse and worse and worse:
Work froze and furloughed,
Friends and family nursed then hearse'd,
Civil Rights hit a reverse,
And it seemed like all of 2020 was cursed—
But You— You're still placing First.

Discipline was asked of You.
Patience got the best of You.
Traumas truly challenged You.
And You still made it through.

.... I am oh so proud of You.

If the battle hasn't shown You
That your demons cannot own You,
Then I don't know what to tell You...
... Your tenacity is a virtue.

So I'm thankful You're still here.
Yes, we can celebrate this year.
More was asked of us than ever before— My dear:
You deserve a toast... Cheers.

ALL THAT I'VE BEEN THROUGH KEPT ME HUMAN.
ALL THAT I'VE GAINED MADE ME A GOD.

Kashiya Lester is an artist, life coach, and spiritual counselor, using her writing gifts to share insight and wisdom gained through her own personal journey. Hailing from Wilmington, Delaware, Kashiya's entire mission is to help others understand, and succeed within their own spiritual journeys, without as much unnecessary pain as she, herself, endured. Using rhythmic and expressive form, Kashiya seeks to express some of the more intimate parts of Ascension, and connect with readers far and wide.

'Her Psalms' is not just Kashiya's story, it is every woman's story.